MoRe
ThAn
Teä A
PArTy

MORE THAN A TEA PARTY

JANE EVERSHED

HarperSanFrancisco
A Division of HarperCollinsPublishers

Harper San Francisco and Jane Evershed, in association with the
Rainforest Action Network, will facilitate the planting of two trees
for every one tree used in the manufacturing of this book.

Library of Congress Cataloging-in-Publication Data

Evershed, Jane
    More than a tea party / Jane Evershed. — 1st ed.
        p. cm.
    ISBN 0–06–251125–4 (pbk.)
    1. Evershed, Jane, — Themes, motives.   2. Greeting cards—United States—Themes, motives.   I. Title.
    NC1868.E93A4 1994
    741.6'84'092—dc20   94–11261

94 95 96 97 98 ❖ GLO 10 9 8 7 6 5 4 3 2 1
This edition is printed on acid-free paper that meets the American National Standards
Institute Z39.48 Standard.

 Printed on recycled paper.

This book is dedicated to my daughter,
Elizabeth Mattingly,
may her strong spirit never be broken, and to my son,
Evershed Mattingly, may he grow up to be a loving, nurturing man.

Preface

When I was nine years old my family left England on a six-week ocean liner voyage. Our destination: South Africa. We disembarked into a separate world, a closed-off white enclave from which I would emerge years later in horror. I was so sheltered I had never even heard of the African National Congress (ANC) until I left school. In my early twenties I volunteered to teach art to Zulu children. Each week I crossed through distinct racial borders, a Nazi palette of urban planning and control known as apartheid. As a white person, I knew I was inextricably a party to the brutal oppression of a people who couldn't even move freely in their own land. This realization was a cathartic turning point in my life and was the primary catalyst for my work as a socially conscious artist.

After the birth of my son, I decided we should leave the country. At that time it was mandatory for white males to serve in the South African army, so to stay was to commit his future to white supremacism. Also, I had been jailed once for activism and, given my political stance, I was certain it would happen again. I realized therefore that I could be more effective furthering the cause of freedom from outside the country. My very first paintings, the Dream for South Africa series, expressed a vision of peace and justice for the land I loved, but could no longer rightfully call my home. Years later I realized racism is everywhere, white South Africa just gave it an official name—apartheid.

In 1984, when I was twenty-five years old, my son and I came to live in Minnesota with his father. The long, dark winters were a brutal shock compared to the warm subtropical climate in which I had grown up. I was far from family and friends and felt desperately alone. As a homebound housewife and now mother of two, it became clear that the career of the man of the house took precedence over mine. Here *my* freedom was at stake, yet I refused to surrender my spirit. My only outlet from the never-ending monotony of domestic duties and society's expectations of women was my art. Guided by the flying women that emerged in my paintings, I began to soar, invoking new heights of consciousness through my Power of Women series.

Another series, You and I, We Are the Majority, voiced the parallels I saw between the oppression of the African people and that of women worldwide. Exploring deeper into the domination of women, I then realized that this same mind set is responsible for the rapacious violence against nature. My reaction to these injustices resulted in the Scarred Sacred Earth, Animals Crying, and Realm of the Nurturing Man series.

I am convinced that when we as women reclaim our full ancient powers and when men awaken to their loving and caring nature, a balanced society respecting all life is truly possible. My work stands in affirmation to this belief.

—Jane Evershed, Spring Solstice, 1994

I like my bed
to be

Outside under a tree.

JANE

African Beach Party.

You and I
We are the majority
We don't want war
Fun undermines authority!
JANE

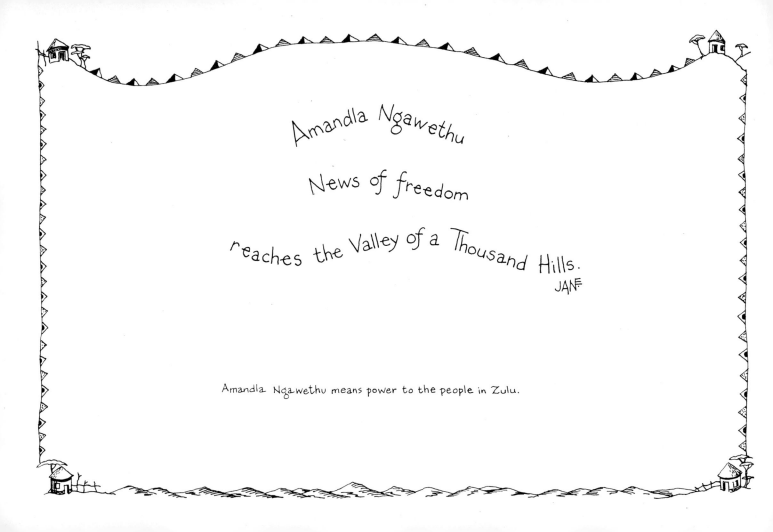

Amandla Ngawethu

News of freedom

reaches the Valley of a Thousand Hills.
JANE

Amandla Ngawethu means power to the people in Zulu.

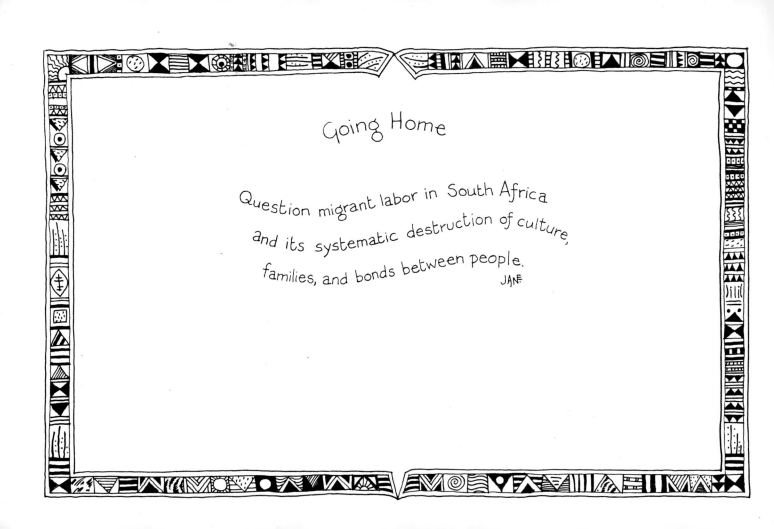

Going Home

Question migrant labor in South Africa
and its systematic destruction of culture,
families, and bonds between people.

JANE

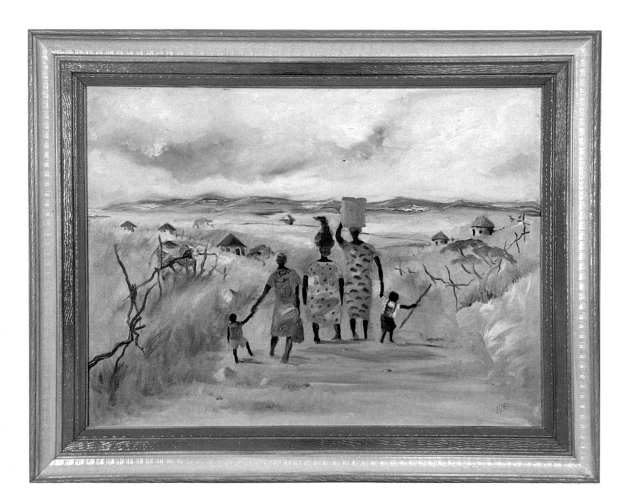

African Mirage.

I wish I could take Africa by the hand and lead her to unity
away from those who seek to destroy her as she stands
But I would have to be a Goddess of Supreme Diplomacy
Such as this world has never known
Since Africa herself erupted
So strong of chest and collarbone

Never dreaming she could be dethroned
Never dreaming she could die alone.

JANE

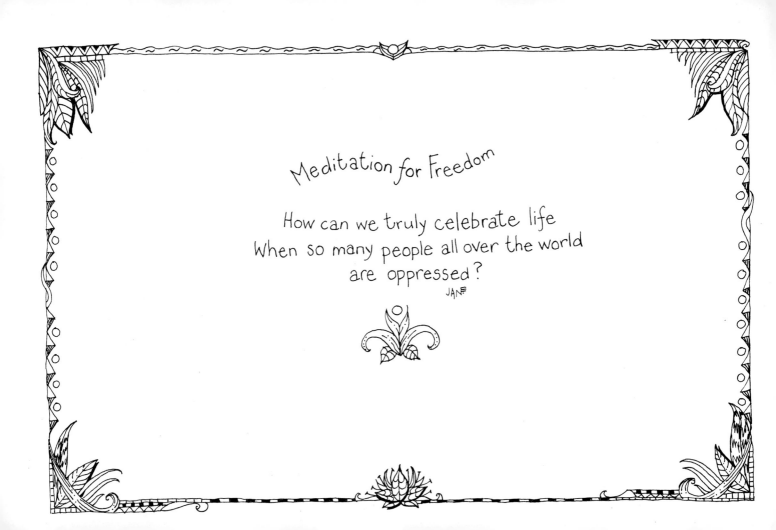

Meditation for Freedom

How can we truly celebrate life
When so many people all over the world
are oppressed?

JANE

Celebration

of

Culture

JANE

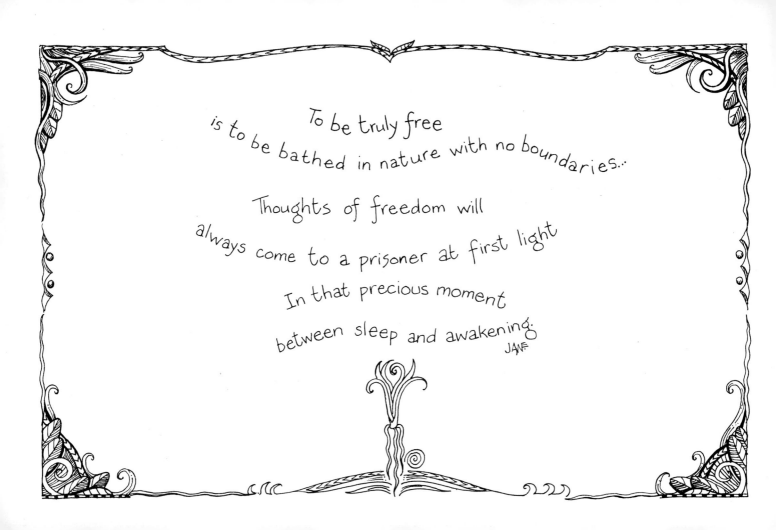

To be truly free
is to be bathed in nature with no boundaries...

Thoughts of freedom will
always come to a prisoner at first light

In that precious moment

between sleep and awakening.

JANE

The People who live closest to the Earth

Treasure the Remaining tribes
Aborigine, Zulu, Cheyenne
All the stolen gold in Africa
Could not buy this wealth of culture,
This dignity of great and noble tribes
Cast aside like empty beer cans
On country roads
Beauty and love woven into beadwork
Khoi-San wiped out for hot-rods and roadwork.

JANE

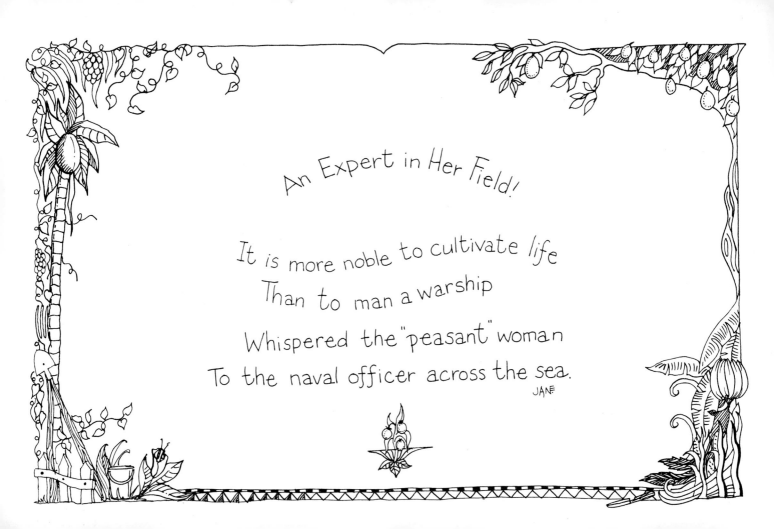

An Expert in Her Field!

It is more noble to cultivate life
Than to man a warship

Whispered the "peasant" woman
To the naval officer across the sea.

JANE

Women with the wave.
Some of the women
chose to chase the wave
whilst others preferred
to ride it.

JANE

Women on the Wind...

Allow yourself strange unacquainted delights
Quintessence spent in experiment
Touching Paradisical heights.

JANE

WOMEN ON THE WIND V

More than a Tea Party!

The women soon realized
That once they had become
One with Mother Earth
She would set them free
And they no longer had to deal with gravity!

JANE

THE WOMEN SOON REALISED THAT WHEN THEY BECAME ONE WITH MOTHER EARTH, SHE WOULD SET THEM FREE, AND THEY NO LONGER HAD TO DEAL WITH THE FORCE OF GRAVITY

Picnic With Nature

Pick a balmy day in summer
Your picnic cloth weaves tight threads
of camaraderie with nature —
— and your selves.

Floating, feeling, focusing through the soft haze
Your reality moves slowly into view
The shadow below now a memory
Forgotten in a newfound joviality.

JANE

ANY WOMAN WHO HAS PRESERVED HER INDEPENDENCE THROUGH ALL HER SERVITUDES WILL ARDENTLY LOVE HER OWN FREEDOM IN NATURE · SIMONE DE BEAUVOIR · 1936 ·

If Women Could Move Mountains...

They wouldn't!

What's the point?

Mountains look great

Just where they are!

JANE

Forest Fantasy

Oh to be woman

And dance naked and fearlessly

with Mother Nature.
JANE

Women in the Woods

We shall dance forever
In the forests of our dreams
Till the sweet breath of life
enables us to thrive
In the labyrinth of true justice.

JANE.

Let me fly free

Away,

Away,

...from the shackles of domesticity.

JANE

LET ME FLY FREE, AWAY, AWAY FROM THE SHACKLES OF DOMESTICITY

Women walking on the edge

How do your tea leaves lie?
As randomly as violence against women?

By night I wear a mask and go with vigilance along the edge
By day I dream of tenderness
Your torments are shared to me in whispers
And by your brother's insistence
You extinguish your flames of violence with your own breath
I feel my disappointment and rage dissipate into a fearless dance
I am no longer denied my creativity

My lust for life is strong and enduring
My cup is full, the tea leaves matter no more. JANE

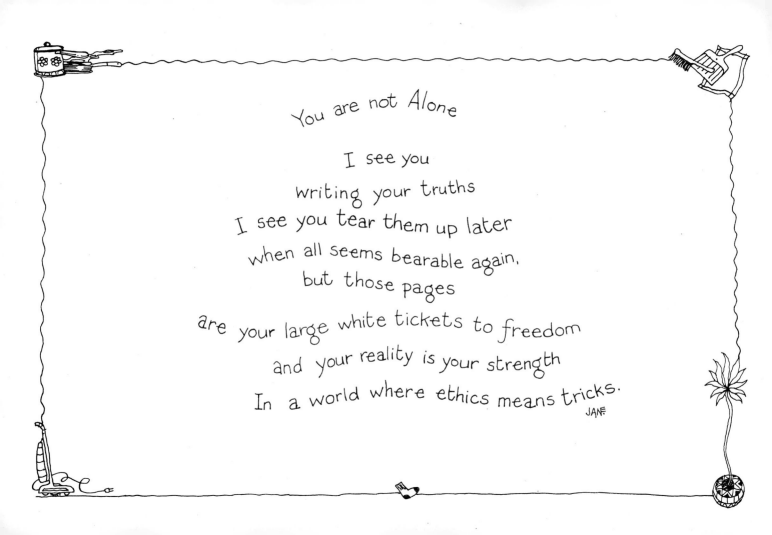

You are not Alone

I see you
writing your truths
I see you tear them up later
when all seems bearable again,
but those pages

are your large white tickets to freedom
and your reality is your strength
In a world where ethics means tricks.

JANE

Truth Visiting
Be prepared
To risk everything you hold precious
for the truth inside you.

Truth is empowering
And to speak the truth
is to overcome the fear of death

and on the other side of hell

lies paradise.
JANE

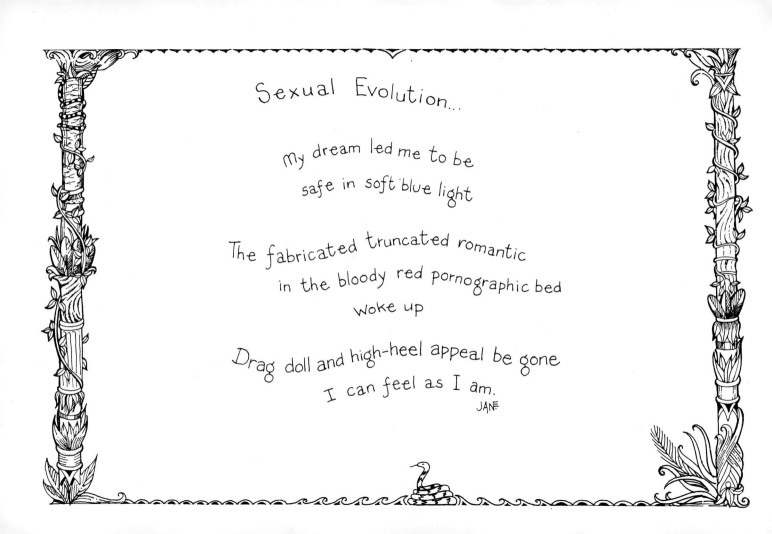

Sexual Evolution...

My dream led me to be
safe in soft blue light

The fabricated truncated romantic
in the bloody red pornographic bed
woke up

Drag doll and high-heel appeal be gone
I can feel as I am.

JANE

Sometimes...

She could be found daydreaming

In the corner of her room

Where she could not be touched.

JAN

She could not be reached

I go where no man has trod before
Where no system can follow
A place where passion awaits
Those who meditate beyond
The barriers of superficial

Man~made dreams.

JANE

The Great Leap of Faith

It's yours — take it!

Leap like a lunatic
Over the chasm below
Erupting as you go
Your true self awaits you
Now, you will know.

JANE

Women Reading

To read is to **empower**
To empower is to **write**
To write is to **influence**
To influence is to **change**
To change is to **live**

JANE

Many Voices, One Vision.

Sisters of the great parade,
We have bannered our way
Through centuries of risk and ridicule
Our grass roots have become giant redwoods
gathering strength over time
bracing against those who would fell us
without thought of our contribution to this world

Our trickle has become the powerful river of change
giving sustenance and hope to all living beings

We know that each community we work with worldwide
accords an ounce of peace
on which to build a planet of peace.

JANE

Commissioned in 1994 by the U.S. League of Women Voters to commemorate sufferage,
celebrating 75 yrs of a woman's right to vote.

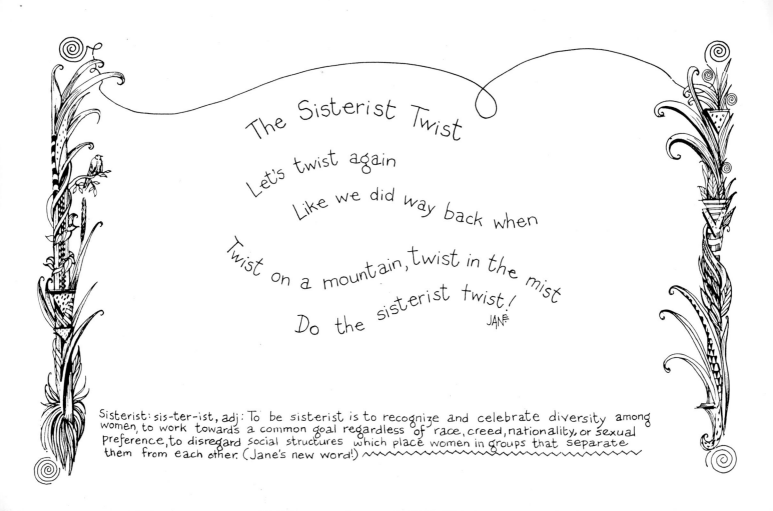

The Sisterist Twist

Let's twist again
Like we did way back when
Twist on a mountain, twist in the mist
Do the sisterist twist!

JANE

Sisterist: sis-ter-ist, adj: To be sisterist is to recognize and celebrate diversity among women, to work towards a common goal regardless of race, creed, nationality, or sexual preference, to disregard social structures which place women in groups that separate them from each other. (Jane's new word!)

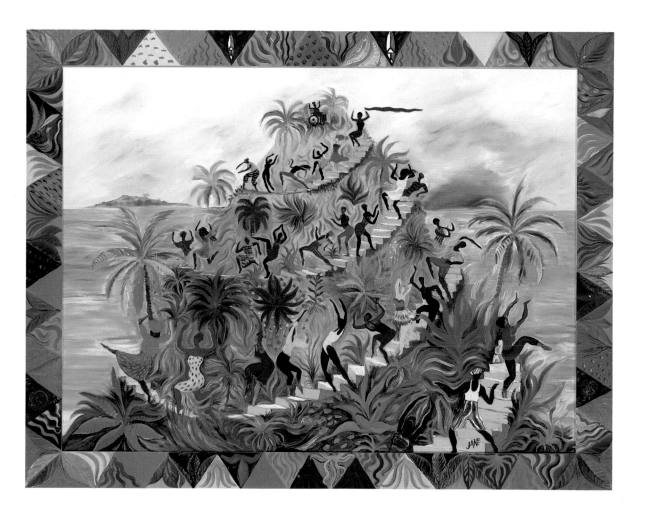

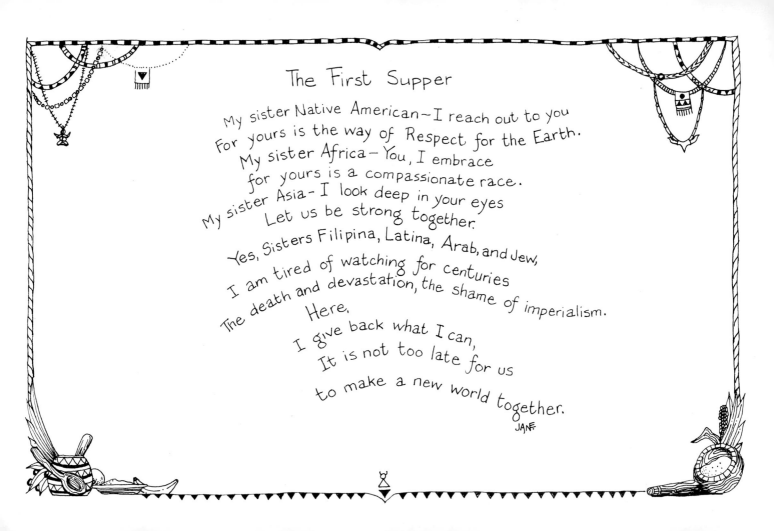

The First Supper

My sister Native American — I reach out to you
For yours is the way of Respect for the Earth.
My sister Africa — You, I embrace
for yours is a compassionate race.
My sister Asia — I look deep in your eyes
Let us be strong together.
Yes, Sisters Filipina, Latina, Arab, and Jew,
I am tired of watching for centuries
The death and devastation, the shame of imperialism.
Here,
I give back what I can,
It is not too late for us
to make a new world together.

JANE

A Woman's Choice

I cannot allow
All the years of my life
To rest upon my brother's decision

Neither do I consider myself
Superior to any other species on earth
I decide for myself.

JANE

The Virgin

My friend told me
" The true meaning of Virgin is—
A woman unto herself
or a soul~mother"
and I like that!

JANE

The Journey

Traveling for a thousand years
over unyielding, unfamiliar terrain
I chanced one day upon our touch
which was at once

The core of the Earth and the edge of the universe
Awakening in a sea of liquid flesh

the waves rushed over me
and carried me home at last.

JANE

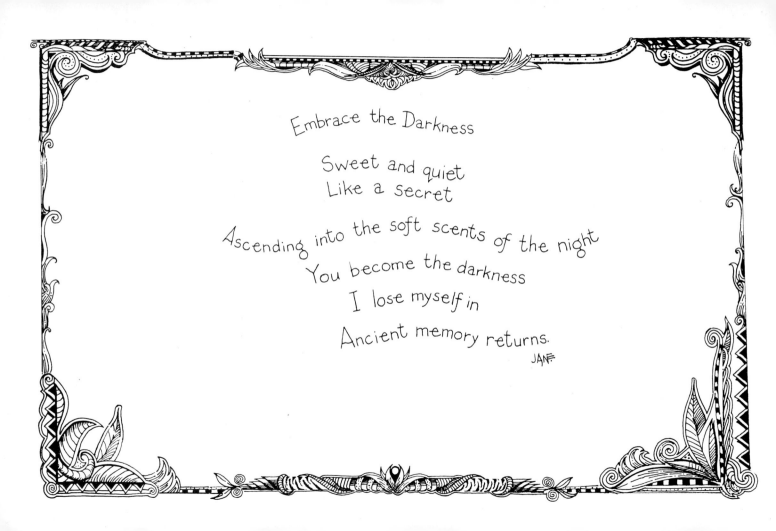

Embrace the Darkness

Sweet and quiet
Like a secret

Ascending into the soft scents of the night
You become the darkness
I lose myself in

Ancient memory returns.

JANE

The River of Life

Heightened emotions
Charged by the moon

Silver strands of menstrual wisdom
women have webbed for centuries

waving and dancing
Like seaweed anchored to an aqua seabed

My round belly a planet
moving among the heavenly bodies
No shame or filth or curse is this
It is the earth, the moon, and me
In harmony.

JANE

Hey Pssst! — The Witches are back

In their millions, these good wholesome women
are hell~bent on the abrupt halt
of this ugly, poisonous, unstimulating man-made environment
They are brewing sweet concoctions
to heal our scarred sacred earth
Riding high in the sky
On broomsticks of sisterhood wood
They cackle with glee
into the next century.

JANE

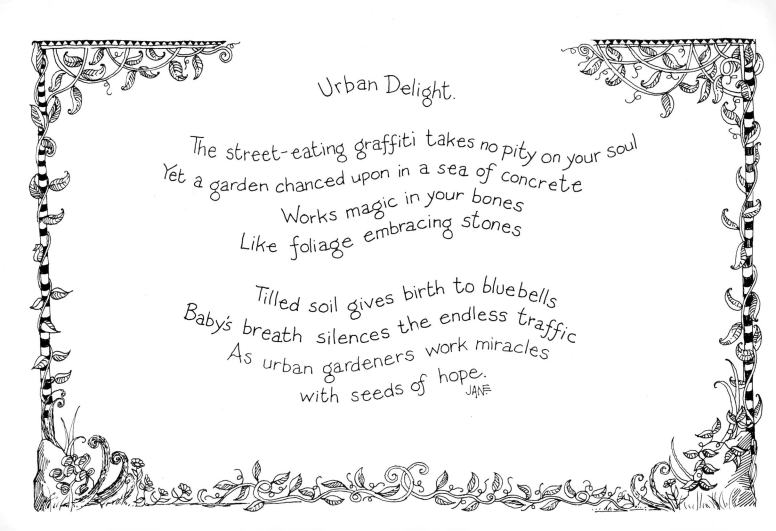

Urban Delight.

The street-eating graffiti takes no pity on your soul
Yet a garden chanced upon in a sea of concrete
Works magic in your bones
Like foliage embracing stones

Tilled soil gives birth to bluebells
Baby's breath silences the endless traffic
As urban gardeners work miracles
with seeds of hope.
JANE

Eight Lane Highway Blues.

Please don't destroy all the lovely old places.
Rolling along the winding road no more
They blew a chasm into my neighborhood
A highway of speeding metal that cuts like a knife
Through the soul of my community
For every speeding motorist, a crack house
Where once there was a winding road.

JANE

PLEASE DON'T DESTROY ALL THE LOVELY OLD PLACES

The Winds of Truth carry a message in their Whisper.

Listen to the wind...

We must learn to share the beauty of the Earth
for to fight over it
is to destroy it anyway.

JANE

A Pocket of Peace.

I imagine that peace moves like quiet Sunday morning sunshine
Across a tidy little room in a house
And then away over the countryside
After a heavy snowfall has settled

I hear peace sound like chimes
reaching you on the wind
from a green and purple front porch

I imagine that peace feels like
An absence of conquest
A psyche that knows no shame
And carries the ultimate knowledge
that a planet of peace is born
of the merging of many pockets of peace.

JANE

High Drama On Planet Earth

Though I walk seemingly alone
Bouncing back from brutalities
Reeling from wars and destruction
Refusing to hold the cold hand
of the geocidal patriarchy

My stride is lengthened   My soul strengthened

To know

That your goal also
is that sunlit glade of sanity
where visions of clarity
and actions of healing abound.

JANE

Contamination of dreams

Where are **your** reactors?
Volcanic eruption or
Total nuclear destruction?

No second chances
<u>Everything</u> goes
from sanity to spiders
All the water, every grain of sand
Give me more candle light at night
Let's make our own music,
Grow gardens again.

JANE

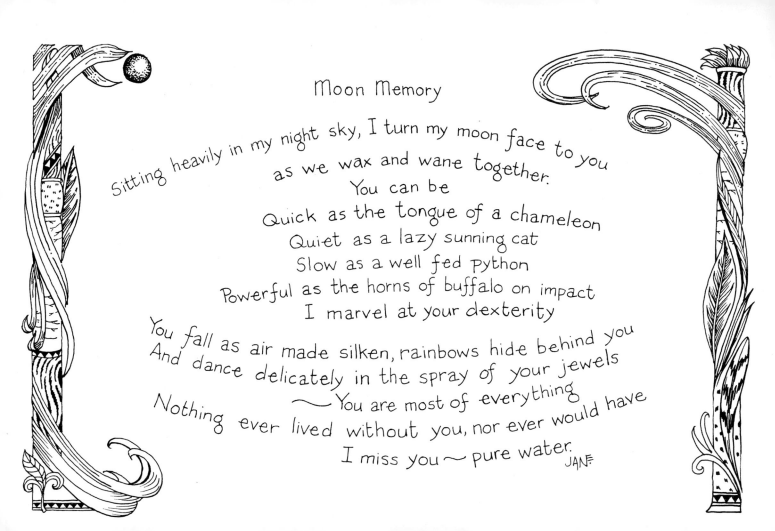

Moon Memory

Sitting heavily in my night sky, I turn my moon face to you
as we wax and wane together.
You can be
Quick as the tongue of a chameleon
Quiet as a lazy sunning cat
Slow as a well fed python
Powerful as the horns of buffalo on impact
I marvel at your dexterity

You fall as air made silken, rainbows hide behind you
And dance delicately in the spray of your jewels
～ You are most of everything
Nothing ever lived without you, nor ever would have
I miss you ～ pure water.

JANE

Mourning in the Rainforest.

If trees could scream
no one on Earth would
sleep peacefully
again.

JANE

Earthdance

Let our inner eye see
The invisible damage
Let our hands repair broken ecosystems

Let our inner ear hear
The snapping of food chains
And let our hearts respond
not just to the oil on the rock
but to the Earth's biological clock.

JANE.

Dance for Mother Earth's Infinity

Respect Mother Earth
and she will feed, clothe and shelter you

Destroy her
and she can only show you a wasteland

where spring flowers
are a distant memory.

JANE

The Garden of Eden revisited.

Had we walked the

path of nurturing together,

Counseled among each other
As equals

for the good of our children,
the Earth and all species...
Would Eden still exist?

JANE

from: Revisiting Our Souls series.

A Strange Phenomenon!
(men listening)

Now that the monster of patriarchy
is turning upon itself
And devouring its own tale
Our true fathers can return
with long-awaited gifts of love.

JANE

It may be...

That the magical formula

for a balanced, conscious, and responsible society

is gender equality in the arts of nurturing

and governing.

JANE

Respect

Respect leaves a note for a
sleeping woman
saying that all is well
It brings a warm blanket
if she is cool to the touch

Respect tidies the tools of work and play
It sweeps clean the sacred fireplace
And patiently repairs fine lace

Respect is love honored, it looks you in the eyes
and tells only truth, it will not live with lies
Respect bonds people in a rhythmic song
As deep as the ocean cleaving to the moon
As strong as a mother suckling her young
I wish respect were more often sung

JANE

Embrace all unions
of love

Love is superior to hate

JANE

The Ribbon of Love

Is a dream

worth holding on to.

JANE

The ribbon of love is a dream worth holding on to.

We have nothing if we have nothing
for our children

You ask me to shoulder your world
I am but a child
and without your care
I am nothing

And when you are weak
and time has almost passed you by
I shall not recognize your cry
for you have taught me to ignore it.

JANE

Peace On Earth 🌙

Good will toward women and children.

JANE

" I swear by my pink walls,

Ain't nobody gonna put <u>me</u> in no institution! "

JANE

Animals Orbiting Earth

Wild animals orbit Earth
In search of a space
to thrive
Like the clouded leopard
Who does not roar
And hunts at night
to survive.

JANE

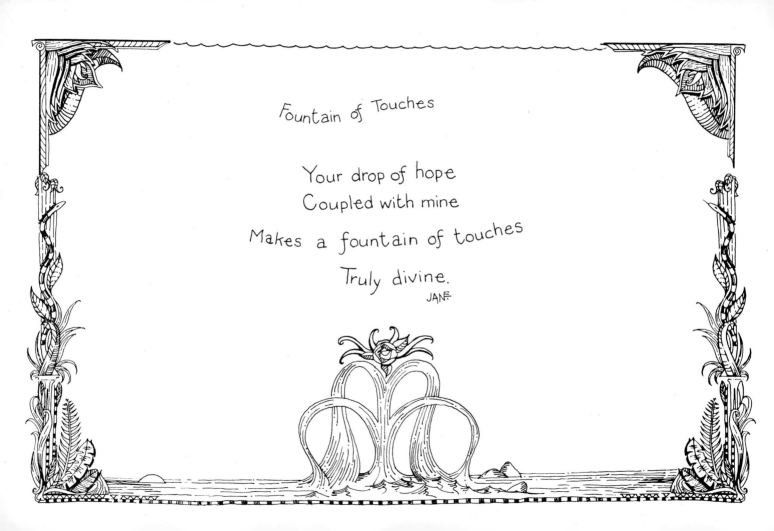

Fountain of Touches

Your drop of hope
Coupled with mine

Makes a fountain of touches

Truly divine.

JANE

Ballet in the Cemetery

What is a deadline~?
But a row of gravestones with

" Rest in Peace "

etched into each cold hard face.
I would not tear myself from
the throes of passion for a date
with a deadline~ Would you?

No one can kiss you when you stand on the other
side of a dead~line~ Do the dance of life!

JANE

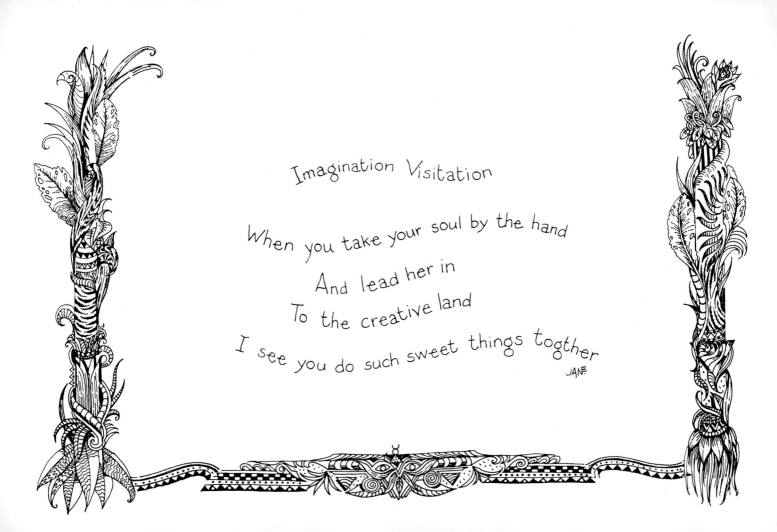

Imagination Visitation

When you take your soul by the hand

And lead her in
To the creative land
I see you do such sweet things togther

JANE

Tickets for two?

I reserved you a seat
In the theater of my life

Please don't fall asleep
during the performance.
JANE

On Facing the Challenge...

...Nobody warned me
my life
would turn into a movie.
JANE

Acknowledgments

My art would not be possible without the love and support of many individuals, among them: my Auntie Rene for insisting that I would grow up to be a famous artist; Mrs. Duck and Miss Lello, my art teachers in South Africa, for awarding me the coveted art prize for nine consecutive years; John King for standing guarantor for a loan for one year of art at the Durban Technikon; the Zulu people for teaching me to keep a sense of humor through the hardest of times; Michael Mattingly for making me canvases out of the trash when I had no money for such luxuries; Terry Smith for photographing and archiving my work without ever asking for a dime; Scott Cramer of Northern Sun Merchandising for printing my very first note cards; Simone de Beauvoir, Andrea Dworkin, and Mary Daly for providing me with a ticket to autonomy and freedom; Cathleen and Colleen McGuire for their radical ecofeminist visions; and my mother, Millie Martens. I would also like to thank my editor, Lisa Bach, for realizing my work is indeed more than a tea party!

The art and poetry in this book are for sale as note cards, book marks, gift bags, large prints, and a journal. This is how I support myself and my two children as a single mother. All my art is printed on recycled paper, most of it chlorine and dioxin free, using soy inks. A compact disc of music and songs inspired by my paintings is also available. It's called *Jagadamba* and features my poems and meditations. If you can't find my work at your local card or gift shop, write to me at the Jane Evershed Card Collection, P.O. Box 8874, Minneapolis, MN, 55408, USA.